THE COWBOY'S OWN BRAND BOOK

THE COWBOY'S OWN BRAND BOOK

DUNCAN EMRICH

ILLUSTRATED BY AVA MORGAN

THOMAS Y. CROWELL COMPANY · NEW YORK

DESIGN BY EDWARD A. HAMILTON

Manufactured in the United States of America
by the Vail-Ballou Press, Inc., Binghamton, New York

LIBRARY OF CONGRESS CATALOG CARD NO. 54-5536

First Printing

For a Young Cowboy

Duncan Gibbons Stearns

Contents

How to Read a Complete Brand   1

How to Read Single Letters   5

The Numbers   26

The Figures   34

Picture Brands   51

Warning Brands   57

Rustlers' Brands   59

How to Design Your Own Brand   63

How to Keep a Brand Book   69

Oh, come along, boys, and listen to my tale,
I'll tell you 'bout my troubles on the old Chisholm Trail,
I rode up the trail April twenty-third,
I rode up the trail with the Bar U herd. . . .

Introduction

In the days when there were no fences in the West, the best means of identifying cattle was to brand them with a hot iron. Even today, when cowboys of different ranches work together at the Spring and Fall roundups, the only way of sorting the cattle of one ranch from those of another is through the special marks of the cattle brands burnt on the hide. Cattle wander great distances, and they cannot speak for themselves to say that "I belong to rancher Jones in Wyoming," or "My range is in Nevada." The brands speak for them.

The act of branding, of course, hurts the young calves at the time, but the pain is very brief—and once the mark or brand is made, it never disappears. The brand cannot be rubbed off. Snow or rain will not wash it off. It is there forever, a permanent mark of ownership and identification.

In the United States, the first people to use cattle brands were the Spaniards who explored California, New Mexico, Arizona, and parts of Texas, Nevada, and Colorado long before we were a nation. The Spanish brands were very complicated and rich in design, like the heavy armor which the explorers wore. They were the brands of Spain, and they did not become the brands of America.

American cowboys and pioneers learned about branding from the Spaniards, and also from the Mexicans. The pioneers saw the need for brands, and how useful they could be. But instead of the complicated brands of Spain, with their rich frills and curlicues, the cowboys and pioneers in the West made their brands simple and direct, very strong and forceful. They were as different as night and day, as different as armor and buckskin.

AN EARLY SPANISH BRAND
IN CALIFORNIA

AN AMERICAN COWBOY BRAND
IN CALIFORNIA

The American cowboys made their brands simple, because they were easier to make and easier to remember. A cowboy out on the range easily remembered a Circle and an A, and he could brand a stray calf with that mark. It was not as easy for him to remember the frills which the Spaniards gave to their letters.

So, with the first American pioneers in the West, and with the cowboys, we have the beginning of American cattle brands. They are part of the history of the wild West, and the brands are known to cowboys in all the Western states—from Wyoming to Texas, and from Kansas and Nebraska to California.

How to Read a Complete Brand

EACH brand is simple to the real cowboy. But a tenderfoot can make many mistakes with brands. In the first place, the tenderfoot does not know how to *read* a brand. And you have to be able to read the brand in order to say the name of the brand aloud.

There are definite rules for the reading of brands, just as definite and fixed as the reading of the words on this page. You are reading these words from left to right. If you tried reading them from right to left, they would not make sense. And if you tried spelling them from right to left, they would make still greater nonsense. The words "real cowboy" would appear as "yobwoc laer"—which, of course, means nothing. So it is important to know how to read cattle brands correctly.

There are three rules for the reading of brands.

Cattle brands are read:
  1. from left to right;
  2. from top to bottom;
  3. from the outside to the inside.

Here are some examples.

Reading from left to right:

2-X
TWO BAR X

P⊰
P LAZY Y

◇/J
DIAMOND SLASH J

Reading from top to bottom:

2/X
TWO BAR X

P⊰
P LAZY Y

◇/J
DIAMOND SLASH J

Reading from the outside to the inside:

CIRCLE A

BOX X

DIAMOND O

These are the three most common ways of making and reading the complete cattle brand. Whenever brands are made in these three ways, they must always be read according to the cowboys' rules and the custom of the West.

The brands are never read from right to left, or from the bottom to the top, or from the inside to the outside. A "Circle A," for example, Ⓐ is always a "Circle A." It is never called "A Circle." An "A Circle" brand would be something quite different, and would look either like this: **AO**, or like this: **A̱O**.

Remember the cowboys' three rules!

How to Read Single Letters

You know the way in which the complete brand is read. You know
the right and wrong way of reading it, and the correct place to begin
reading the brand—from the left, the top, or the outside.

The next step in the understanding of brands is the reading of the
single letters, numbers, marks, and designs. Each one of these is part
of a complete brand.

There are many different ways of making even a single letter, which is one reason why cattle brands are never dull. They are always as interesting and as amusing as puzzles.

Let's begin with the letter R.

The letter R, standing upright, is read simply as R. It is just plain R, and nothing else. It is not doing anything.

But the cowboy did things to his letters. He changed them, and made his own cowboy alphabet. He took the letter R, for example, and branded it as though it were falling over either backward or forward. And he called it Tumbling R.

Then he branded the letter R lying down on its back, and he called it Lazy R. It can face in either direction.

Then he stood it on its head, also facing in either direction, and he called it Crazy R.

CRAZY R

Then he turned the letter around, facing in the wrong direction, and called it Reverse R.

REVERSE R

And he put wings on the letter, and called it Flying R.

FLYING R

And feet on it, and called it Walking R.

WALKING R

And when the feet dragged, he called it Drag R.

DRAG R

And to make a Running R, the cowboy simply wrote the letter out in freehand style, the same way you would write it—not print it—with chalk on a blackboard. It is not a block letter, but a running letter.

RUNNING R

R BENCH

ROCKING R

SWINGING R

R QUARTER CIRCLE

Then the cowboy did still other things with the letter R. When it was standing on a bench, he called it R Bench. This is all one figure, joined together.

The same thing is true of this figure, which the cowboy called a Rocking R. It is all one figure. The letter R is rocking on the quarter circle to which it is joined.

By joining the quarter circle to the top of the R, the cowboy also made a Swinging R.

When the quarter circle is not joined, however, the brand is read from the top to the bottom, according to the rule. This brand is an R Quarter Circle, and cannot be mistaken for a Rocking R.

And this brand is a Quarter Circle R. The difference between it and a Swinging R is very clear.

In the same way that the cowboy combined the letter R with the Quarter Circle, he also combined it with other figures. We will come to many of these different figures later, but we can look at two of them now. The first is a Half Diamond R. The second, at first glance, looks almost the same, but notice that the lines are a little closer to the R and are spread wider. The second brand is called a Rafter R, because the two lines over the R are sloping like the rafters of a cowboy bunkhouse on a ranch in the West. The lines of the Diamond rise to a much higher peak, and that is the easy

QUARTER
CIRCLE R

HALF
DIAMOND R

RAFTER R

way of telling the difference between the two. A tenderfoot, of course, could not tell the difference. He would probably not know how to read either one.

THE RUNNING LETTERS

RUNNING R

You remember the Running R brand. It was written in freehand style, and not printed like a block letter. When you write a letter as a running one, your pen or pencil does not leave the paper. It runs from the beginning of the letter to the end.

Now some letters cannot be running letters. You cannot make a Running X, because you lift your pencil to cross the lines. And some other letters are much easier to make in the plain or block way than in the running way. A plain H brand, for example, is much easier than a Running H. So, as a general rule, the cowboys made running letters only out of those which can "run" naturally and easily. These are some of the cowboys' favorite running letters:

H

H

RUNNING H

RUNNING A

RUNNING B

RUNNING M

RUNNING N

RUNNING R

RUNNING W

RUNNING Y

THE UP AND DOWN LETTERS

CRAZY R

CRAZY F

CRAZY A

When you stand certain letters on their heads, they do not go *completely* "crazy" the way the letter R does or the way the letter F does. Certain letters are simply upside down. The letter A, for example, is just upside down. If it stands alone, it is still, of course, called Crazy A. But if it is with another plain A, and follows it, it is called A Up A Down. These are the Up and Down brands:

A UP A DOWN

T UP T DOWN

U UP U DOWN

V UP V DOWN

Y UP Y DOWN

THE LETTERS M, W, H, I, AND X

The letters M and W cannot be either crazy or up and down, because as soon as you stand an M on its head, it becomes a W, and a W becomes an M. And if you stand an H, an I, or an X on its head, nothing happens. They remain the same, and they cannot be crazy or up and down either.

THE LETTER O, OR THE CIRCLE BRAND

Because the letter O is a circle, it is read as a circle, and not as the letter O. These brands are all circle brands:

M
M
W
W
H
H
I
I
X
X

O
THE CIRCLE
BRAND

CIRCLE X

CIRCLE M

CIRCLE RUNNING B

CIRCLE LAZY L

OR

CIRCLE A
NOT
OA

You can never be wrong if you call the letter O a circle. That is what the cowboys call it. It is a favorite brand of theirs. And a Circle A brand, for example, also sounds more western than a plain O A when you say it.

The letter O can, of course, be used in a brand. Suppose a rancher's name is Bob. That is a short name, and makes a good brand. The brand will be the B O B brand, but the cowboys, instead of reading the letters, would call it the "Bob" brand for short. The letters spell a word, and they would read the word in this case. They would not be wrong, though, to call it the B Circle B brand, because the O can always be a circle.

BOB

THE "BOB"
OR
B CIRCLE B
BRAND

The cowboy had fun with the Circle brand, too, just as he did with all the other letters. He could not make it into a Crazy Circle, because the circle does not change when you turn it upside down, but he could make a Rocking Circle, a Swinging Circle, and a Rafter Circle. And there was one thing he could do to it which he could not do to any of the other letters. He could mash it down, as though it had been sat upon. Then he called it either the Mashed Circle or Goose Egg brand. Both names are correct. It is a Mashed Circle, and it does look like a Goose Egg. You may use whichever name you prefer, or you may use both. Some brands, like the Mashed Circle or Goose Egg, have a double reading.

ROCKING CIRCLE

SWINGING CIRCLE

RAFTER CIRCLE

THE MASHED CIRCLE OR GOOSE EGG

To repeat what has been covered so far:

1. Brands are read from left to right, top to bottom, and from the outside to the inside.

2. The single letters are made in many different ways—Lazy, Crazy, Rocking, Swinging, Running, Walking, Tumbling, and so on.

3. Certain letters are combined to make Up and Down brands, and all letters may be used with the Circle, the Half Diamond, and the Rafter brands.

Here are a few brands giving some of these combinations. The reading is given with each brand.

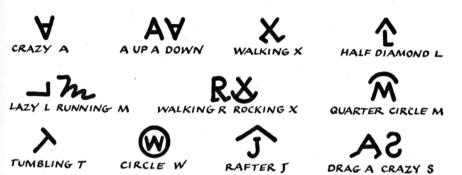

CRAZY A   A UP A DOWN   WALKING X   HALF DIAMOND L

LAZY L RUNNING M   WALKING R ROCKING X   QUARTER CIRCLE M

TUMBLING T   CIRCLE W   RAFTER J   DRAG A CRAZY S

And here are some brands used on cattle ranches today. The correct reading for each brand is given at the bottom of the next page.

1   2   3   4   5

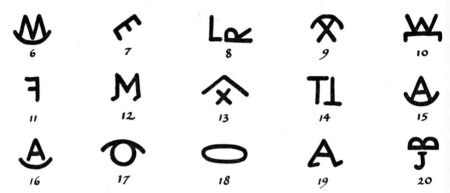

1) Circle D. 2) Half Diamond X. 3) Running B. 4) Quarter Circle B. 5) Crazy F. 6) Rocking M. 7) Tumbling E. 8) L Lazy R. 9) Swinging X. 10) W Bench. 11) Reverse F. 12) Drag M. 13) Rafter X. 14) T Up T Down. 15) Rocking A. 16) A Quarter Circle. 17) Swinging Circle. 18) Mashed Circle, or Goose Egg. 19) Walking A. 20) Lazy B J.

Before we leave the letters, there are just one or two things more about them which all cowboys know, and which you have probably already discovered for yourself.

The first thing is simple: the cowboys' letters are always capital letters. In all of the brands that you have seen and read so far, there are no small letters. Even the Running letters are all capitals. The cowboys could, of course, have used small letters if they had wanted to, but for some reason they never liked them. And the reason probably is that the big capital letters make better designs, and are also easier to make in the first place. A Tumbling E looks like a Tumbling E, but if you try to make a Tumbling E out of the small letter, it begins to look like something else. It becomes hard to identify, and hard to read. The capital letters are strong and big, like the West. They are easy to read from a distance.

The second thing is also simple, and it is something which you will discover about the different letters as you begin to make your own designs and brands. You know that the letters H, I, and X cannot become Crazy letters, because when you turn them upside down, they remain the same. And letters like X or H cannot be used as Running letters for brands, while certain other letters, like M, W, B, and R are good for that kind of brand. You will find, then, that some of the letters can do certain things which other letters cannot.

There is no rule here which you can follow. It is simply a matter of plain western horse sense and practice.

Just by way of example, though, try to make a Walking I or Walking T or Walking L. You cannot do it, because they are not two-legged letters like A, R, K, M, and N. They cannot walk. Try also to make a Lazy I. You can do it, but it looks too much like a Bar, and the cowboy does not use a Lazy I because it would be confusing. Also, a Flying A is easier to make and read than a Flying S. A Flying S begins to look like some other design entirely. It does not look like an S at all.

FLYING A

?

There is no exact rule to follow about this. From practice, however, you will soon discover the right and the wrong. Try always to make the brand clear and unmistakable.

On these two pages are the readings for twenty-one cattle brands. Design the brand in pencil above each reading, and then check the designs against the brands on pages 24 and 25.

REVERSE E   TUMBLING T   FLYING M

WALKING X   DRAG A   RUNNING W

U UP U DOWN   CIRCLE R   QUARTER CIRCLE B

SWINGING B   B QUARTER CIRCLE   ROCKING B

M BENCH   GOOSE EGG   RAFTER L

HALF DIAMOND L   LAZY R L   LAZY R LAZY L

And now make a Circle F in three different ways. Remember the
three rules.

CIRCLE F   CIRCLE F   CIRCLE F

REVERSE E

TUMBLING T

FLYING M

WALKING X

DRAG A

RUNNING W

U UP U DOWN

CIRCLE R

QUARTER CIRCLE B

SWINGING B

B QUARTER CIRCLE

ROCKING B

M BENCH

GOOSE EGG

RAFTER L

HALF DIAMOND L

LAZY R L

LAZY R LAZY L

And the three Circle Fs:

CIRCLE F

CIRCLE F

CIRCLE F

The Numbers

Cowboys use numbers to make brands in the same way that they use letters. The numbers may stand alone in a Tumbling or Lazy position; or they may be combined with a letter, as in the Six R brand—6R; or they may be combined with figures like the Rafter, Quarter Circle, Circle, or Bench.

The same rules that apply to the letter R, for example, can be applied to the number 2, or to any other number.

You can make a Lazy Two,

or a Rafter Two,

or a Tumbling Two.

You can make a Five Bench,

or a Rocking Six,

or a Circle Three,

or a Seven Quarter Circle.

Whatever you have done with the letters, you can do with the numbers—provided, of course, that the brand is a clear one and easy to read. Remember that the Flying S did not make a particularly clear brand, because it began to look like something other than an S. The same thing holds true for the numbers. A Flying Three begins to look like something else. The Three does not make a good Flying number. But the number Eight makes a fine one, just as the letter A did.

FLYING
EIGHT

So when you make the different numbers in their different positions, you will find that some numbers turn out well and that others do not. When the number is clear and recognizable—whatever its position—it is a good brand. When the number is not recognizable, it becomes hard to read, and therefore it is not a good brand.

THE NUMBER ONE

Because the number One can easily be confused with the letter I, cowboys are usually careful to brand them so that they will be unmistakable.

1
THE ONE
BRAND

They do not make either the One or the I tumble, because then they begin to look like a Slash. And they do not make them Lazy, because then they look like a Bar. They usually make them upright—a plain One and a plain I—in order not to confuse them with the Slash or the Bar.

I
THE I BRAND

/
SLASH

—
BAR

THE ZERO

M CIRCLE TWO

The Zero, like the letter O, is a Circle. It is always a Circle, and should be read as a Circle. The brand on the left, for example, is an M Circle Two, and not an M Zero Two.

As far as the Zero is concerned, there is only one exception to this rule. (There are always exceptions to rules!) When a brand is clearly a "number" brand, then the Zero keeps its value as a number, and does not become a Circle. It should be read as a number. This brand is clearly the One Hundred brand, and even a cowboy would feel foolish reading it as the One Circle Circle brand. The Sixty brand, also, is a full num-

ber, and it would be going out of your way to read it as a Six
Circle brand.

The same thing holds true for the Nine Hundred Nine,
or Nine-Oh-Nine, brand. You would not read it as a Nine
Circle Nine.

909
NINE
HUNDRED
NINE

But whenever the Zero is combined with letters or figures
—like the Rafter or Bar—it is always read as a Circle.

O−
CIRCLE
BAR

BRANDS WITH TWO NUMBERS

Any brand with two numbers can be made in the same way
that you would normally write the numbers on paper, and
it is also read in the same way. The Twelve brand or the

12
TWELVE

92
NINETY-TWO

Ninety-two brand are very clear and simple, and look just like the numbers as you always see them.

But the cowboy liked to make interesting designs with the numbers whenever he could. With the Seventy-six brand, for example, he found that he could join the slanting line of the Seven to the line of the Six to make a single design instead of having the two numbers stand separately. He still read the brand, though, as the Seventy-six brand, because it stands for the two numbers.

76
SEVENTY-SIX

Ƶ
SEVENTY-SIX

With other numbers, the cowboy could do the same thing. Here are some of the ways cowboys have joined two numbers in different brands which have been used in the West.

6̸3
SIXTY-THREE

8̸6
NINETY-SIX

4̸6
FORTY-SIX

4̸4
FORTY-FOUR

2̸4
TWENTY-FOUR

4̸5
FORTY-FIVE

7̸4
SEVENTY-FOUR

4̸7
FORTY-SEVEN

7̸5
SEVENTY-FIVE

56
FIFTY-SIX

2̸7
TWENTY-SEVEN

5̸2
FIFTY-TWO

The Figures

AFTER the letters and numbers come certain figures, or designs, which are very common in the cattle country, and which are known to all cowboys. These figures are used alone, and also in combination with the letters and numbers.

The figures are the Bar, the Slash, the Box, the Circle, the Diamond, the Triangle, and the Heart. This is a good place to gather these brands together and see what the cowboy can do with them

The Bar is a straight line, and not very long. It is usually no wider or longer than any letter. If it is much longer, it is not called a Bar, but is called a Rail. The Bar always lies on its side. If it were upright, it would look like a number One or the letter I.

BAR

The Rail is much longer than a Bar, and is usually used by itself without being combined with any other letter, number, or figure. It was an early Texas brand, but is not common or popular now, because a long brand like the Rail burns too much of the hide. The hide is valuable for leather, so the big brands are not used.

RAIL

The Slash looks like a Bar, except that it is always drawn

SLASH

U. S. 939532

at an angle, leaning either to the left or right. It looks something like a Tumbling I or Tumbling One, but is never called that. It is always the Slash, and cowboys use it a great deal.

The Box looks like a square, but cowboys prefer the word Box and always call the brand by that name. When the Box is open at one side it is called an Open Box brand. Usually, also, a letter or number stands inside the Box or Open Box as in the two brands on the left.

By adding lines to the four corners of the Box, the cowboys made a brand which looks something like the four rail fences of a small pen or enclosure. They called this the Pigpen brand.

The upper quarter of the Box the cowboys used, but called it a Bench, because it looks like the wooden benches in front of the bunkhouses in the West. The other quarters of the Box they do not use, because they begin to look like the printed or block letter C, and do not look like part of a Box.

BENCH

CIRCLE

MASHED CIRCLE, OR GOOSE EGG

We already know about the Circle brand, and also that it can become a Mashed Circle or Goose Egg brand. It can also be used as a Quarter Circle in four different positions, using any one of the four quarters. When the Quarter Circle is joined to a letter from above, the letter becomes a Swinging letter; and when the Quarter Circle is joined below, the letter becomes a Rocking one.

QUARTER CIRCLE

SWINGING X

ROCKING X

HALF CIRCLE X

X HALF CIRCLE

QUARTER MOON

HALF MOON

BUCKLE

SUN

The Circle may also be divided into Half Circles, in order to make, for example, a Half Circle X, or an X Half Circle

And when the Quarter and Half Circles have an added line to make them appear like moons, they become the Quarter Moon and Half Moon brands.

Also, when a full circle has a line drawn in it from top to bottom, it looks like an old-fashioned, round buckle, and is called by cowboys the Buckle brand.

And when the circle has small lines pointing outward from it that look somewhat like the rays of the sun, the brand becomes the Sun brand.

Diamonds are always drawn or branded either as the full

Diamond, or as a Half Diamond. There cannot be a Quarter Diamond, because the quarter of a diamond is a single line, which looks exactly like a Slash.

When a Half Diamond is joined or connected to the lower part of a full Diamond, the cowboys call the brand the Diamond and a Half brand.

The Half Diamond is usually the upper half of the diamond, but it can also be drawn from the two sides to make, for example, a Half Diamond S or an S Half Diamond. The bottom half of the diamond cannot be used, because it is the letter V.

Before leaving the Diamond, there is just one more thing

about it—or about the Half Diamond—which needs explaining. When you read the Half Diamond in a brand which reads from top to bottom, it is always the Half Diamond. The brand at the left is a Half Diamond S. But when the Half

HALF
DIAMOND S

Diamond stands on a level with the S, in a brand which is read from left to right, then the Half Diamond is called an

OPEN A S

Open A. It looks like an unfinished A, without the cross bar. If a rancher's name, for example, is Alfred Adams, and he

A OPEN A

wants to use the two initials of his name for a brand, and yet make them different in the brand, he can make an A Open A brand.

TRIANGLE

The Triangle brand is a very simple one, and the three

lines of the triangle can be drawn so that the triangle is either standing on its base or on one of the points. The cowboys like to place a letter or number in the triangle, just as they do with the box and circle.

TRIANGLE S

The Heart brand is not as common as the Circle or Diamond, but it is still quite popular with the cowboys and can be found on many ranches.

The cowboy changed his heart, too, and made it Lazy or Crazy if he felt like it. And then, also, if he happened to be broken-hearted over something at the time when he chose his brand, he could select the Broken Heart brand for his cattle.

HEART

LAZY
HEART

CRAZY
HEART

BROKEN
HEART

We have covered the letters, the numbers, and the commonest figures. One more thing, and we can go on to the reading of a hundred brands. This one thing is quite simple. It involves the joining, or connecting, of letters, numbers, and figures in the making of a brand. For example, we know that the Box H is made in three different ways:

BOX H   BOX H   BOX H

But there is still another way to make a Box H, which is like this:

BOX H

The difference is clear. In the last brand, the H is joined or "connected" to the Box. Now cowboys, when they make a "connected" brand, simply read it as a straight brand—in this case, a Box H. They very rarely use the word "connected." But they do occasionally use it when there is any doubt about the brand. Suppose that one ranch in Wyoming has a Box H brand which is made like this: ▣ , and a nearby ranch also has a Box H, but made like this: ◻H . Then the cowboys will always call the last one a Box H Connected, simply to distinguish it from the first. When there is no need to distinguish it, however, the cowboys do not use the word "connected." So you may use the word "connected" if you want to, but there is no real reason for doing so unless there is doubt about the brand and a need to distinguish it from another "unconnected" brand.

The cowboys themselves do not often use it, so we will not use it either, except in special cases.

Here are the hundred brands:

A
A

AA
DOUBLE A

a
RUNNING A

AⱯ
A OPEN A

AⱯ
A UP A DOWN

A-B
A BAR B

$\frac{A}{B}$
A BAR B

A∞
A LAZY B

CIRCLE A

 BOX A

 OPEN BOX A

 A BENCH

 DIAMOND S

 HALF DIAMOND S

 RAFTER S

 TRIANGLE X

 DIAMOND AND A HALF

 DIAMOND A

 DIAMOND A (CONNECTED)

 YJ (CONNECTED)

 Y SIX

 XE

 XE (CONNECTED)

 SWINGING N BAR

B DOUBLE BAR

 DOUBLE BAR ROCKING R

 A RUNNING M

 FOUR SIXES

 SLASH LAZY R

CIRCLE 5 X

 FLYING SIX

TUMBLING T BAR

 REVERSE E NINE

W DIAMOND

 CIRCLE BAR

 H CRAZY Y (CONNECTED)

 S R (CONNECTED)

OPEN A BAR R

 GOOSE EGG

 PIGPEN

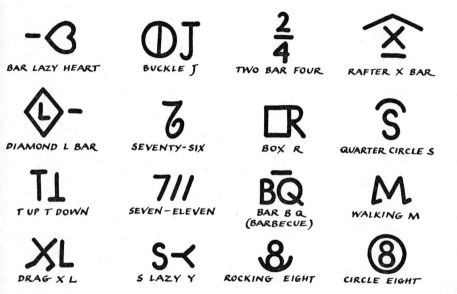

BAR LAZY HEART

BUCKLE J

TWO BAR FOUR

RAFTER X BAR

DIAMOND L BAR

SEVENTY-SIX

BOX R

QUARTER CIRCLE S

T UP T DOWN

SEVEN-ELEVEN

BAR B Q
(BARBECUE)

WALKING M

DRAG X L

S LAZY Y

ROCKING EIGHT

CIRCLE EIGHT

ROCKING CIRCLE
EIGHT

SWINGING C

FIVE SLASH R

FLYING M E

S BAR S

QUARTER CIRCLE
X BAR

QUARTER CIRCLE
X BAR

QUARTER CIRCLE
X BAR

HALF DIAMOND
A BAR

TRIANGLE SEVEN

CIRCLE ELEVEN

J F

CRAZY R R

U UP U DOWN

RUNNING B FOUR

TUMBLING A

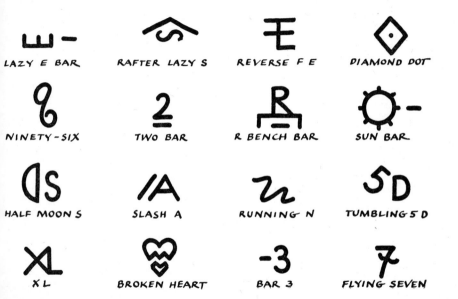

LAZY E BAR

RAFTER LAZY S

REVERSE F E

DIAMOND DOT

NINETY-SIX

TWO BAR

R BENCH BAR

SUN BAR

HALF MOON S

SLASH A

RUNNING N

TUMBLING 5 D

XL

BROKEN HEART

BAR 3

FLYING SEVEN

FORTY-FIVE

WALKING A BAR

CRAZY P E

REVERSE P E

TUMBLING H

LAZY 2 Z

FOUR SLASH N

SWINGING L BAR

QUARTER CIRCLE U

LAZY K L

X SLASH Y

Picture Brands

You have had the brands with letters and numbers, and also with the basic designs of the Diamond, Circle, Box, Triangle, and Heart.

You have also had a few "picture brands." You have had the Sun, the Quarter Moon, the Buckle, the Pigpen, the Half Moon, and the Goose Egg. Each one of these brands you read as a "picture," and not as letters, numbers, or designs.

SUN

QUARTER MOON

BUCKLE

The cowboys like picture brands, and they are found on many cattle ranches in the West. The picture brands are chosen or made by ranchers and cowboys for different reasons. A rancher, for example, might be very proud of the first

CABIN, OR
HOUSE

cabin or house built on his ranch, and for that reason choose the Cabin or House brand. Or a cowboy in Montana, living

HAT CREEK

on Hat Creek, might make the Hat Creek brand, which would be an address and a brand at the same time. A rancher

SUNRISE

who liked the sunrise over the mountains in the West might make the Sunrise brand. And another rancher whose name happened to be John Bell could very easily make the J Bell

J BELL

brand.

Cowboys also made brands of the various things which they saw on their ranches, such as Pitchforks, Spur Rowels, Bridle Bits, Steer Skulls, and other objects.

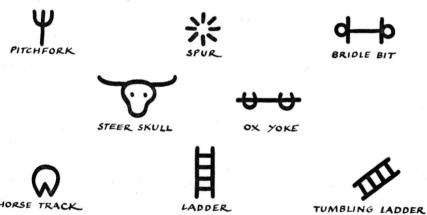

PITCHFORK

SPUR

BRIDLE BIT

STEER SKULL

OX YOKE

HORSE TRACK

LADDER

TUMBLING LADDER

DOLLAR SIGN

QUESTION MARK

When they hoped to make money from their ranch work, the cowboys might take the Dollar Sign as a brand. And if a rancher were doubtful about making a success of ranching during the heavy storms of winter or the dry days of summer, he might very easily take the Question Mark for a brand. Once he had taken the brand, it would be his forever, and the doubtful Question Mark might thus become the brand of a very rich ranch, while the hopeful Dollar Sign might wind up representing a very poor outfit.

There are many reasons, as you see, for choosing picture brands. Also, of course, cowboys chose some of them simply because the designs pleased them and were easy to remember.

Here are more picture brands which have been used on western cattle ranches.

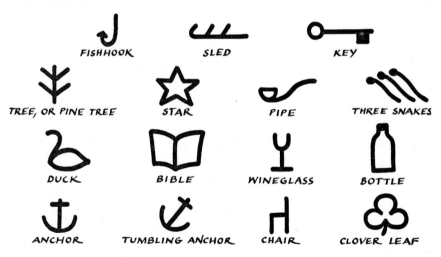

FISHHOOK   SLED   KEY

TREE, OR PINE TREE   STAR   PIPE   THREE SNAKES

DUCK   BIBLE   WINEGLASS   BOTTLE

ANCHOR   TUMBLING ANCHOR   CHAIR   CLOVER LEAF

Ψ
PITCHFORK L

3 Ω
THREE BELLS

Picture brands usually are used alone, because they are complete in themselves, but sometimes they are used with letters and numbers. A Pitchfork L, for example, makes a good design. Also, a rancher might want the Three Bells brand, and instead of branding all three bells, he would simply put a three before the bell.

And if a rancher's name happened to be Barker or Barkey, he could very easily make a brand which could be read as his full name.

BARKER

BARKEY

Warning Brands

In the early days of the West, there were, as you know, cattle rustlers who stole cattle from the ranches and sold them as their own, or changed the brands and kept the cattle for themselves. Cattlemen and cowboys warned these rustlers that there would be trouble for them if they touched the cattle of their ranches—and they warned them with brands on the cattle. Suppose a rustler, for example, were to see the ICU

I-U
I BAR YOU

2-U
TO BAR YOU

.45
.45

brand. He would know at once that the cowboys of the ranch were ready and waiting for him, and he would think twice before trying to rustle cattle from that ranch. The I Bar U brand, and the 2 Bar U brand also give the same warning signal. They tell the rustler to "keep hands off!" Perhaps the strongest warning brand, though, in the days of the old West, was the .45—which was the symbol for the cowboys' .45 Colt revolver. The rustler who touched that brand knew at once that he was heading for real trouble—and gunsmoke. It would be a foolhardy band of rustlers who tried to run the cattle off. Not far away, and ready for trouble, were cattlemen and cowboys with Winchesters and Colts.

Rustlers' Brands

Rustlers, of course, had no real brands of their own to start with. They simply changed other brands until they were un-recognizable, and called these brands their own. They had to build on already existing brands. Suppose a rustler lived near two ranches, and one of the ranches had a Chair brand, and the second ranch had an Eleven brand. The rustler could change both of these brands into the Rocking Chair brand with a very few lines.

CHAIR

ELEVEN

CHAIR   ROCKING CHAIR   ELEVEN   ROCKING CHAIR

This is how it was done.

Many other brands can be changed in the same way, simply by adding a Slash or a Bar, or making some basic change in the design.

RUNNING AND FIXED IRONS

In order to control the cattle brands and to put a stop to the rustlers' work, the cattlemen and cowboys in the West established certain rules about branding. They outlawed the use of the running iron as a first step.

The running iron was simply a short rod, about the length of a fire poker, which the cowboy carried attached to his saddle when he was riding the range. Whenever he saw a stray calf without a brand, he roped it, built a small fire, and "ran" the brand of his ranch upon the calf. You can see how easily, though, with a running iron a rustler could change any brand. So the running iron was outlawed, and any cowboy caught carrying a running iron was immediately suspected of being a rustler. He had to prove that he was not—otherwise he was in serious trouble.

A RUNNING IRON

In place of the running iron, the cattlemen agreed that all branding irons should be "fixed irons." This meant that the full brand had to be designed and fashioned by the ranch blacksmith, in a fixed form, and soldered to the end of th iron. Thus the brand became a stamp. It could not b changed by stamping another brand over it. The differenc between a "running iron" and a "fixed iron" is exactly th same as the difference between making a brand with a penci on a piece of paper and stamping the same brand on pape with a rubber stamp. The brand made with a fixed iron i always the same, and never varies. Every rancher could easil recognize his own brand, because he knew his iron, and be cause the brand was always exactly the same every time he used it.

A FIXED
IRON

How to Design Your Own Brand

You have seen the many, many ways of making and reading brands, and now you are ready to design your own.

Remember, as a general rule, that brands are made out of one, two, or three figures.

They are almost never made out of more than three figures because the hide is valuable, and cowboys do not want to burn more hide than is necessary.

Also, brands are usually designed to be "open" and not "closed." An "open" brand is one that can be stamped cleanly, without blotching. It is clear, and can be easily read. A "closed" brand is not clear and clear, and often blotches, so that it cannot be read. It also scar the hide badly, and for this reason cowboys do not use the "closed" brands.

A Circle or a Circle X are good "open" brands, but a Circle X Bar or a Target are closed brands, and not good.

CIRCLE   CIRCLE X
(OPEN BRANDS)

CIRCLE X B BAR   TARGET
(CLOSED BRANDS)

You see how easily the last two brands can blotch. They actually close up, and become "closed" brands.

CIRCLE X B BAR

TARGET

Many ranches have more than one brand. A ranch will often have two different brands for the cattle, and a third brand for the horses. So you can design three different brands for yourself also. You can make one of your initials; another one with a figure—like a Circle or Diamond—and one initial; and another out of numbers. You can make all sorts of combinations, and then also you have the "picture" brands to design and choose from.

If, for example, a rancher's initials are H.E., the following are brands that he could design before finally choosing the one from which he would make his iron.

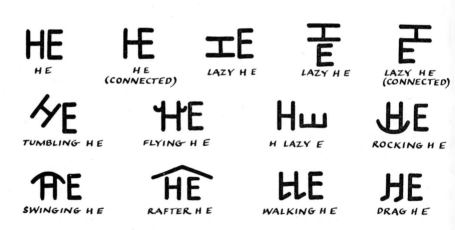

HE

HE
(CONNECTED)

LAZY H E

LAZY H E

LAZY H E
(CONNECTED)

TUMBLING H E

FLYING H E

H LAZY E

ROCKING H E

SWINGING H E

RAFTER H E

WALKING H E

DRAG H E

HE–   HE   ⒽE   H/E
H E BAR   H E BAR   CIRCLE H E   H SLASH E

H–E   H̲   H–Ш   ⫽–Ш
             E
H BAR E   H BAR E   H BAR LAZY E TUMBLING H BAR
                                        LAZY E

If you take your pencil and paper and go to work on it, you will
ee that the rancher has only just begun to design the many possible
rands to be made out of his initials. You can do the same thing with
our initials, using both initials, and then also adding the third
nitial as well (if you happen to have one). And if you add Boxes

and Diamonds, Hearts and Benches, and the other figures, you will begin to see that the total number of designs is almost limitless.

When numbers are used in brands, they are usually chosen for a good reason. You may choose a number because it is the number of your house, or your "ranch." Or you may decide to join two of your friends in starting a "ranch," and because there are three of you, you may choose to identify yourselves with the number Three. If you did this, you might very naturally make a Circle Three brand, or a Rafter Three.

There are many reasons for choosing brands. But the best reasons of all are: 1. that the brand makes a good design, and 2. that it reads well, or sounds like the real West.

How to Keep a Brand Book

WHEN you design brands, you will want to keep a listing of them so that you can find them easily. And you will also want to keep a listing of your friends' brands, so that you can recognize the brands and know at once to whom they belong.

You can do this by keeping a brand book, as the cowboys do.

A brand book is just as orderly as a dictionary, and the brands in it are as easy to find as the words in a dictionary. In a dictionary, the words beginning with A come before those beginning with B, and all the other letters follow in their proper alphabetical order until the last letter, Z. The same thing holds true for brands beginning with letters. So the first thing to do in your notebook—or brand book—is to set aside a page for each letter, except that you skip the letter O, because it is a Circle. The Circle comes in a separate place, and has another page to itself.

All brands *beginning* with A, you enter under the letter A.

All brands *beginning* with B, enter under the letter B.

Then, to make a very complete brand book, enter the reading of the brand, and also the person to whom it belongs. Here are a few examples for the letter A:

BRAND	READING	OWNER
a	RUNNING A	JAMES BROWN
A̲X (A bar X)	A BAR X	HAROLD JONES
∀/	CRAZY A SLASH	ARTHUR SMITH
A⊰	A LAZY Y	ALFRED YOUNG

After making a page for each letter, then make nine pages for the numbers from 1 through 9. Do not enter the Zero, because that will come under the Circle. Here are a few brands for the number Six:

BRAND	READING	OWNER
6̸	SIXTY-THREE	JOE BOWERS
6A-	SIX A BAR	RICHARD ELIOT
6II	SIX ELEVEN	PHILLIP WRIGHT

After you have made pages for the letters and numbers, then make separate pages for each of these common symbols, using one page each for:

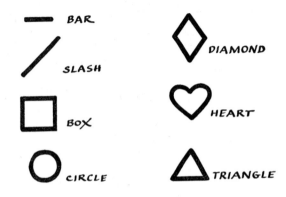

- BAR
- SLASH
- BOX
- CIRCLE
- DIAMOND
- HEART
- TRIANGLE

Any brand *beginning* with a Bar, enter under the Bar. Any brand *beginning* with a Slash, enter under the Slash, and so on. The Bar Double A brand, for example, should be entered on the Bar page, and not on the A page.

When you come to the Half Circles and Quarter Circles, and to the Open Boxes and Half Diamonds, enter them under the pages for Circles, Boxes, and Diamonds, because they are part of the Circles, Boxes, and Diamonds.

Here are a few brands for the Circle page:

BRAND	READING	OWNER
®	CIRCLE R	HENRY STEELE
⟨A⟩	QUARTER CIRCLE LAZY A	BRYAN BATES
⌒M	HALF CIRCLE M	KENNETH BREED

Then, after you have made pages for the letters, numbers, and common symbols, keep a few pages at the end for the "picture" brands.

With a little practice—both by yourself and with your friends—you can quickly find any brand in your brand book. Just remember: first the letters in their order; then the numbers; then the common symbols, like the Bar and Circle; and last, the "picture" brands.

As you use the brand book, you will find that it is as easy as using the dictionary. It will become a real dictionary of brands, and a record of your own brands and those of your friends.

And you will be following the great tradition of the cowboys and of the early West.

YOUR BRAND REGISTER

BRAND	READING	OWNER

BRAND	READING	OWNER

BRAND	READING	OWNER

BRAND	READING	OWNER

BRAND	READING	OWNER

BRAND	READING	OWNER

BRAND	READING	OWNER